MY HEROES, MY PEOPLE

AFRICAN AMERICANS AND NATIVE AMERICANS IN THE WEST

PORTRAITS BY
MORGAN MONCEAUX

TEXT BY
MORGAN MONCEAUX
AND **RUTH KATCHER**

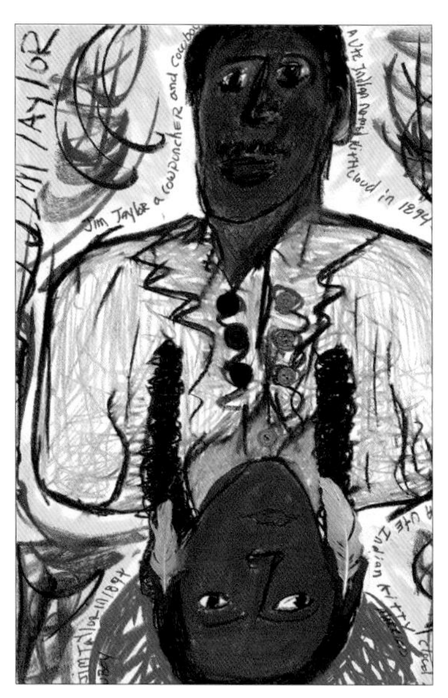

FRANCES FOSTER BOOKS
FARRAR, STRAUS AND GIROUX
NEW YORK

MY HEROES, MY PEOPLE

AFRICAN AMERICANS AND NATIVE AMERICANS IN THE WEST

To my beloved. —M.M.

Acknowledgments

This book would not exist without the patience and vision of Frances Foster and the encouragement of Morgan Rank. We owe an enormous debt to the collections of the New York Public Library, especially the Schomburg Center for Research in Black Culture, and the Brooklyn Public Library. In addition, Ruth Katcher wishes to thank Melinda, Patrick, Charlotte, and Daniel Burke for their friendship during the long process of research and writing, and Jeff Newell, who listens.

Distributed in Canada by Douglas & McIntyre Ltd.
Color separations by Tien Wah Press
Printed and bound in Singapore by Tien Wah Press
Designed by Claire B. Counihan
First edition, 1999

Library of Congress Cataloging-in-Publication Data
Monceaux, Morgan.
My Heroes, My People : African Americans and Native Americans in the the West / text by Morgan Monceaux and Ruth Katcher ; portraits by Morgan Monceaux. – 1st ed.
p. cm.
Summary: Presents brief portraits of an assortment of African Americans, Native peoples, and men and women of mixed heritage who played roles in the history of the American West.
ISBN 0-374-30770-9
1. Afro-Americans–West (U.S.)–Biography–Juvenile literature. 2. Indians of North America–West (U.S.)–Biography–Juvenile literature. 3. Racially mixed people–West (U.S.)–Biography–Juvenile literature. 4. West (U.S.)–Biography–Juvenile literature. 5. West (U.S.)–History–Juvenile literature. [1. Afro-Americans–West (U.S.) 2. Indians of North America–West (U.S.) 3. Racially mixed people–West (U.S.) 4. West (U.S.)–Biography.] I. Monceaux, Morgan, ill. II. Title.
F596.3.N4K38 1999
920.078–dc21 98-45400

CONTENTS

A Note from Morgan Monceaux 7

Introduction: The West 9

THE LEGENDS 10

Montezuma 10 Pocahontas 11 Toussaint L'Ouverture 13

THE FUR TRADE 14

Jim Beckwourth 14 The Bongas 17

THE COWBOYS 18

Nat Love 18 Ned Huddleston 20 Ben Hodges 21

CRIMINALS AND LAWMEN 22

Crawford Goldsby 22 The Rufus Buck Gang 23 Bass Reaves 24

THE STAGECOACH DRIVER 26

George Monroe 26

THE WOMEN 28

Biddy Mason 28 Clara Brown 30 Mary Fields 31

Luticcia Parsons Butler • Elvira Conley • A Mail-Order Bride • Cathy Williams 32-33

BUFFALO SOLDIERS 34

Moses Williams 34

NATIVE AMERICANS 37

Outina 36 John Horse 38 Little Raven 41 Ely Parker 42

Red Cloud 45 Sitting Bull 46 Standing Bear 49 Kintpuash 50 Chief Joseph 53

Cochise 55 Geronimo 57

AFRICAN AMERICANS AND NATIVE AMERICANS UNITED 58

Edmonia Lewis • John Taylor and Kitty Cloud • Diana Fletcher • Juanita 58-59

THE RODEO 60

Bill Pickett 60

A Note on Sources and Further Reading 62

Index 64

A NOTE FROM MORGAN MONCEAUX

I grew up in Louisiana in a time when it was said that if you had just a drop of Negro blood you were black. I was eight years old the summer I learned I was also part Indian.

All that summer, our relatives kept arriving. I think my Great-grandmother Nana knew she was dying, and she called her children and their families to her to pass along her blessing to them. They came from all over: Shreveport, Louisiana; Michigan; and Oregon. The cousins fit right in with the neighborhood kids, and every night after dinner we'd play cowboys and Indians. My friend Larry insisted on being the sheriff, because he had a badge. "There must be law and order in this black town," he'd say.

It was my Uncle George who got us thinking about things. The first time I saw him, he was getting off the train in his cowboy boots and a big Mexican hat. He wore a gun belt but no guns. He was very tall and dark, with a big thick mustache, and when he walked he jangled. He smelled of cigars and rose water and sweat. I learned that night that he was Mama's younger brother. He'd left home when he was thirteen, and had lived in Texas, California, and Mexico, where he owned a ranch.

Uncle George became a hero to us kids that summer. Every night he'd bring out a watermelon and sit down and talk to us about Mexico and its people, and about the West. He held us spellbound with his stories about cowboys and Indians, and our games took on a new life.

He started the other grownups talking, too. Mama told us about the Maroon people–fugitive slaves from the West Indies–in Florida. Our great-grandmother told us her mother was from the great Seminole nation that had once ruled Florida, and she herself was the daughter of a Creek chief. My cousins and I realized then that we had Indian blood in us, too.

One day Papá, my great-grandfather, came out of his workshop to stop a fight between a kid named Renard and my sister Elaine. Renard said there was no such thing as black soldiers in the West. We already knew better, but that day Papá told us about how the black soldiers were called buffalo soldiers because people thought their hair looked like a buffalo's mane.

Later that summer, Uncle Joe and Uncle George took us kids to Texas to see our first black rodeo. We knew about rodeos, but we had never heard of one where all the cowboys were black. I saw bulldogging for the first time. When we got home I tried it on my dog Jeff, and he bit me.

That summer helped me see the connection between our games of cowboys and Indians–and the Wild West of the movies–and a history in which my family had a place. It showed me that our heritage included Native Americans, too, and it sparked my lifelong fascination with the West, which I've tried to capture in these portraits.

INTRODUCTION: THE WEST

Traveling west across the United States, one meets a new landscape beyond the Mississippi. The earth–vast plains, deep gorges, and, eventually, towering mountains–spreads out under an enormous sky. Possibly because of its sheer physical scale, the West has represented something very special to our country. It evokes a sense of movement–thundering herds of buffalo, waves of settlers moving across the land in wagon trains, families and nations of Indian peoples. The West is also inextricably linked to tragedy, having been the stage for some of America's most bitter confrontations.

This landscape and the story of westward expansion occupies a rich and complicated place in the American psyche. For some, the West was the best of this country, symbolizing our strength, our newness, and our ability to make a home out of what seemed to be wilderness. For Native Americans, however, it meant the loss of land and of freedom.

Under the immense Western sky, where humans seem small and insignificant, it takes some effort to realize that the history of the West, like any history, is the story of individuals great and small. Yet these players shaped the land as surely as centuries of wind and rain. Though historical movements are often sweeping in scope, they can also be seen through the eyes of a portraitist, through the experiences of one person and another and another.

This book is a collection of portraits of people of color who were in one way or another significant in the history of the Western United States. Some you will have heard of. Others will probably be new to you. Many lived during what is thought of as the heyday of the Wild West, the first decades after the Civil War. Some lived centuries before that. But through their individual stories, they all represent the fortunes of people of color in a society that was constantly changing, growing, fighting, ever on the move. Like all those who went west to seek their fortunes, like all those displaced by the fortune-seekers, they wanted to find the place where they and their children could prosper, safe and free.

THE LEGENDS

This album begins with people whose lives have become legend. They lived when the Western Hemisphere was being remade, often with violence. As legendary figures, they have come to personify the conflict—and sometimes the alliances—resulting from contact between very different cultures.

MONTEZUMA

The last of the Aztec emperors

c. 1470–1520

Montezuma II reigned over the Aztec empire of four hundred cities and subject territories. His home was the island city of Tenochtitlán—present-day Mexico City—where his family had ruled for over a century. There was no greater king in his world.

In the spring of 1519, word reached Montezuma of intruders who spoke of one true god—in contrast to the many gods worshipped by the Aztec—and another great king. Later that year, an army of strangers arrived in force, led by Hernando Cortés, who had been sent by the Governor of Cuba to explore the land, possibly for conquest. Cortés formed alliances with Montezuma's enemies among the Aztec and easily captured Tenochtitlán. Montezuma died in captivity, and the native population was swiftly brought under Spanish control. Soon the Spanish empire in the Western Hemisphere stretched from Chile to Florida, and slaves, both Native American and African, could be found throughout the colonies.

POCAHONTAS

The Indian princess who became an English lady c. 1595-1617

Pocahontas was ten or twelve years old when English explorers arrived to settle an area that they called Virginia, and which her people, ruled by her father, the chief Powhatan, called the Powhatan confederacy. Powhatan distrusted the settlers because previous expeditions had spread disease among his people and had tried to take slaves.

Many years later, Captain John Smith would write of how he was kidnapped and brought to Powhatan. He said that he would have been killed if Pocahontas had not asked her father to spare his life. Was she acting spontaneously or could she have been coached, her act being a graceful way for Powhatan to avoid a damaging battle with the English? As with other historical events that have grown into legend, we'll never know exactly what happened.

We do know that the conflict continued, and in 1613 Pocahontas was kidnapped by British colonists. Powhatan responded by returning some English prisoners, but made no other move, knowing his daughter was safe. Pocahontas was baptized in 1614 and given the name Rebecca. By now, both sides wanted to end the fighting, and Pocahontas's marriage that year to John Rolfe, a colonist, cemented a truce. Soon after, she gave birth to a son.

The next year, the Virginia Company took Pocahontas to England. She was presented at court, but died of a sudden illness, probably smallpox, before she could return home. John Rolfe eventually settled in Virginia and became a tobacco grower.

TOUSSAINT L'OUVERTURE

"Come and join me, brothers, and fight by our side for the same cause"

c. 1743-1803

The man who led the most successful slave revolt in the New World was a slave who had obtained an education. Toussaint L'Ouverture grew up on a plantation in the French colony of Saint-Domingue, now known as Haiti. Taught to read by the black Catholic priest who had baptized him, and fortunate in having a liberal owner who gave him the freedom of the plantation library, he became widely read. In 1791 he participated in a slave uprising inspired partly by the Enlightenment ideas of liberty and equality that had kindled the French Revolution two years earlier. Rising among the ranks of black leaders, he issued this proclamation in 1793:

> Brothers and Friends: I am Toussaint L'Ouverture. My name is perhaps known to you. I have undertaken to avenge you. I want liberty and equality to reign throughout Saint-Domingue. I am working toward that end. Come and join me, brothers, and fight by our side for the same cause.

Playing the French and Spanish, who had colonized the island's eastern end, against each other, Toussaint gained control of the colony. In 1796 he was made Lieutenant Governor of Saint-Domingue, and in 1801 he issued a constitution that ended slavery on the island and gave him power for life. Although he was arrested soon afterward by Napoleon's French Army and died in prison, the revolution continued after his death. It would be decades before Haiti's freedom was permanent, but the colony became the second self-governed republic in the New World.

THE FUR TRADE

People of various races and nationalities—Native American, French, English, African American—worked together in the fur trade harvesting deer, beaver, and muskrat pelts which were sold in markets around the world. North America's interior seemed a fearsome place to many who had settled along the coasts. It was the fur trappers and traders, navigating by canoe and barge along its waterways, who explored and charted this Northern wilderness.

JIM BECKWOURTH

The slave who became a Crow chief and discovered a passage to the Far West

Like many African Americans in the fur trade, Jim Beckwourth started life as a slave. He was born, probably in 1798, to a white father and an African American mother in Virginia. Later, as a free adult, he worked as a fur trapper and lived among the Crow, eventually marrying a Crow woman and becoming a chief.

While employed by the Rocky Mountain Fur Company in the 1820s, Beckwourth made several trips to California before it joined the United States. He also guided parties of would-be miners to California during the gold rush and was a scout during the Indian wars. Later he discovered a passage in the Sierra Nevada—Beckwourth Pass—which became one of the most important overland routes to northern California. During a long lifetime he, like many other trappers, helped map the continent, paving the way—for better or worse—for waves of settlers from the East.

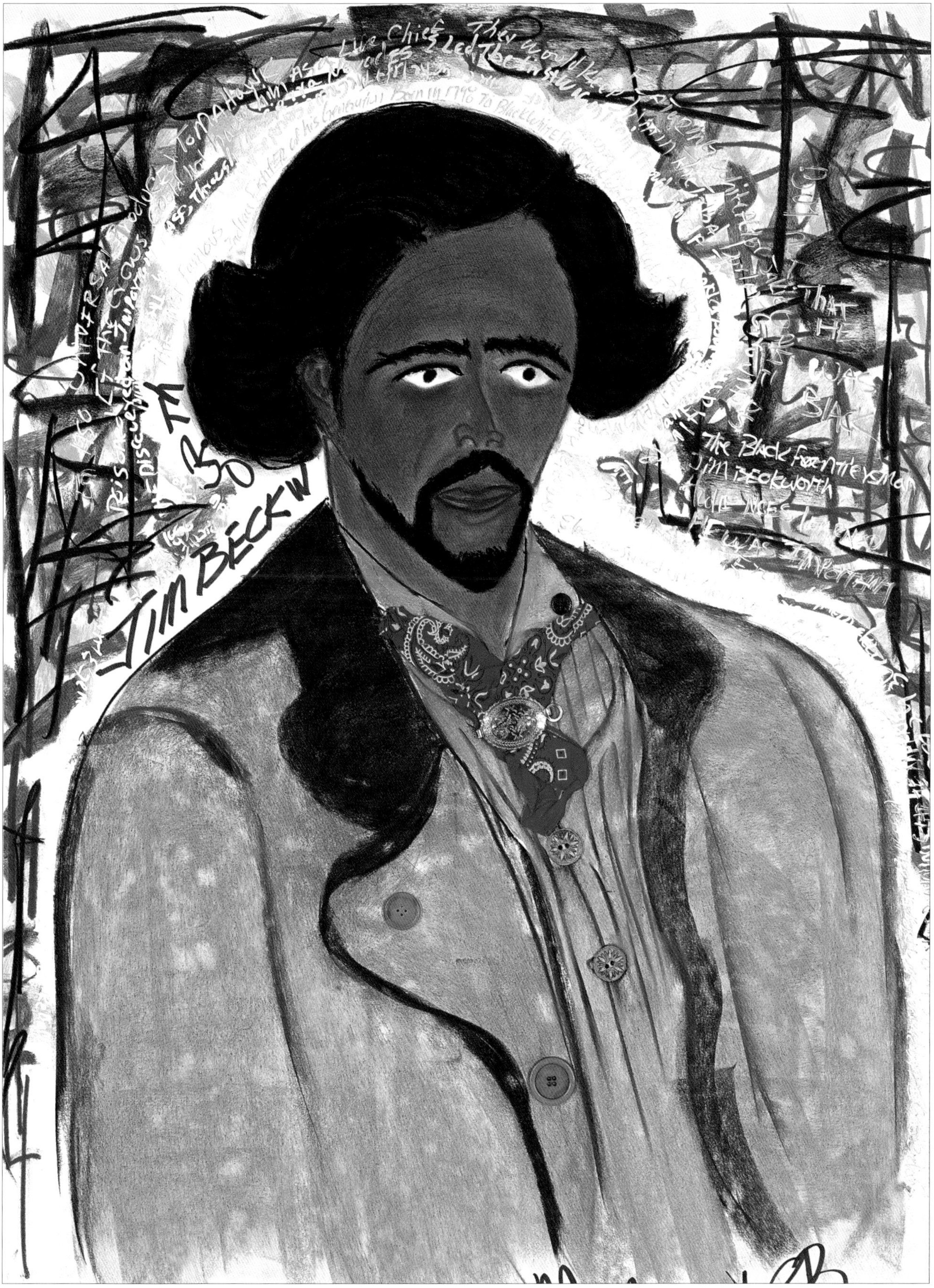
JIM BECKW
The Black frontiersman
Jim Beckwourth

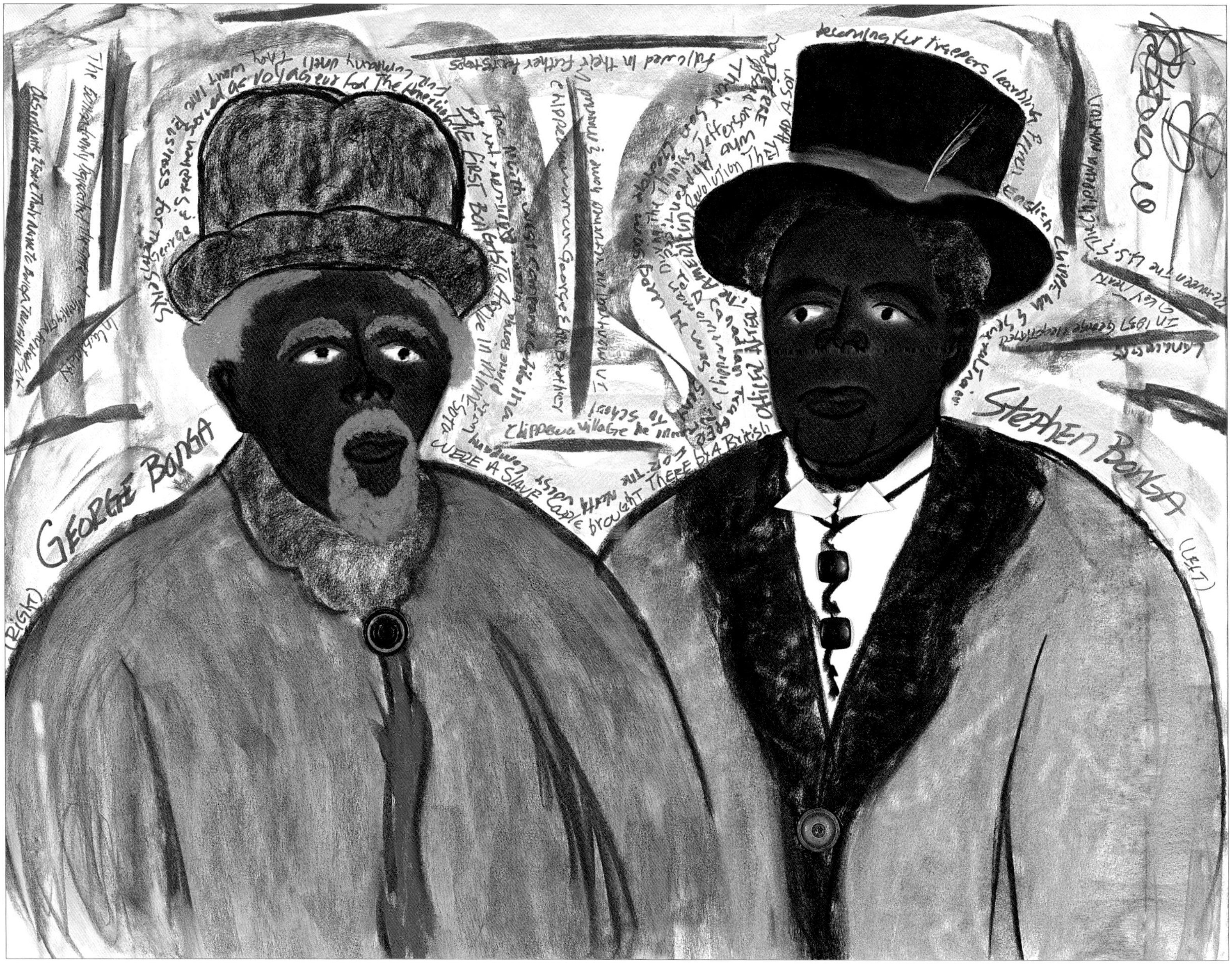
GEORGE BONGA
(RIGHT)
STEPHEN BONGA
(LEFT)

THE BONGAS

"The Indians have had a poor opinion of the government. I must say they have good reasons for it"

The Bonga family were among the most successful and independent African American traders. The best-known, George, born around 1802, was half Negro, half Ojibwa. He wrote in a letter that his father "probably came from the new State of Missouri, as he did not speak anything but French," and his grandfather "might have been taken prisoner by the Indians and sold to the Indian traders."

George and his brother Stephen came from one of at least three generations of traders in their branch of the family. George Bonga was educated in Montreal. He later married a Chippewa woman; in the 1860s he and his sons were still trading in Minnesota.

In 1866, George wrote perceptively about the troubles surrounding settlers, the government, and Native Americans: "I have closely watched the workings of Missionaries amoung the Chippewas to prove to me that an Indian won't try in real ernest to adopt the habits of the Whiteman, before he sees and feels the benefit of civilization...Of late years, the Indians have had a poor opinion of the government. I must say they have good reasons for it."

THE COWBOYS

Possibly the most romantic figure in American history, the cowboy came into his own after the Civil War, when the nation's growing appetite for beef made it profitable to transport cattle–up to 3,000 in a single trail drive–from Texas to the new railroads in Kansas, and from there to points north, east, and west. Cowboys were often uneducated, usually underpaid, and they worked long, uncertain hours. Among their ranks were newly free African Americans who had left the Deep South looking for paid work. Those who had experience with horses were welcome companions on the trail.

NAT LOVE

"I was wild, reckless, and free, afraid of nothing"

In 1869 a fifteen-year-old former slave named Nat Love left his home in Tennessee for Dodge City, Kansas. In a camp outside the city, he approached an outfit of Texas cowboys looking for a job. The camp boss asked if he could ride a wild horse. "Yes, sir," Love answered. The boss told one of the black cowboys to saddle up a horse called Good Eye and put Love on its back.

Years later Love wrote:

> I thought I had rode pitching horses before, but from the time I mounted old Good Eye I knew I had not learned what pitching was. This proved the worst horse...I had ever mounted in my life, but I stayed with him and the cowboys were the most surprised outfit you ever saw, as they had taken me for a tenderfoot, pure and simple. After the horse got tired...the boss said he would give me a job and pay me $30.00 per month...He asked me what my name was and I answered Nat Love, he said to the boys we will call him Red River Dick. I went by this name for a long time.

Nat Love had joined an outfit that, like many others, was made up of both white and African American cowboys. Since some black cowboys had been slaves, and many of the whites were Texans and had been on the Confederate side in the Civil War, there was potential for conflict.

A cattle drive could last for months. During this time the outfit would be isolated, except for other cattlemen they encountered and enemies: outlaws, Indians, or hostile ranchers. Anything that kept the cowboys from working as a team was a serious

problem. And the cowboys knew it.

Many black cowboys, like Nat Love, had worked with horses since childhood and were skilled at riding, roping, and taming wild horses. Slaves from Texas and other frontier states were more likely than those in the Deep South to have worked closely with their white masters. Their experience would be respected, especially during a dangerous stampede or river crossing. After all, the point was to bring the herd to market with as few losses as possible—of men or cattle.

Even so, there were real differences in the status of the white and the Negro cowboys. Their pay might be the same, but a black man would never be a trail boss; it was unthinkable for a white man to take orders from an African American. The exception would be if an outfit was made up of only black cowboys, and even then, a black trail boss might run into trouble with whites encountered on a cattle drive.

The life of a cowhand promised opportunity beyond what was available for most former slaves. After a few years on the trail, Love wrote: "You would not recognize [in] the bronze hardened dare devil cow boy, the slave boy who a few years ago hunted rabbits...on the old plantation in Tennessee...I was wild, reckless, and free, afraid of nothing...with a wide knowledge of the cattle country and the cattle business."

Love was a cowboy for over twenty years. He traveled south to Mexico and north to Nebraska and South Dakota. He learned to speak Spanish, hunted buffalo, and was wounded and then adopted by a Native American tribe, which included several members of mixed race. Nat Love retired in 1890 to work for the railroad as a Pullman car porter.

NED HUDDLESTON

a.k.a. Isom Dart, Tan Mex, Quick-shot, and the Old Black Fox

Not all men who worked with horses and cattle were cowboys. One former slave combined skill with horses with a taste for larceny. Born in 1849, Ned Huddleston traveled to Mexico after the Civil War, working as a rodeo clown—and smuggling stolen horses across the border to Texas. Later, he made a living capturing and breaking wild horses in Colorado, where he drifted into horse thievery, joining a small gang.

After a bloody confrontation with ranchers, Huddleston left town and changed his name to Isom Dart. He lived in Oklahoma for a time, then moved back to Colorado. There he worked as a horse wrangler and operated a small ranch, sometimes taming horses in exchange for livestock. But it seems he couldn't resist rustling cattle as well. One brand he used was the wagon wheel, a favorite of rustlers because it could cover any brand. Like other African Americans in the West, he might have found that ranching offered him a way to be his own boss and make a good living. Dart was killed in 1900 by Tom Horn, a well-known gunman who had been hired by a number of ranchers to stop the rustling near Brown's Hole, Colorado.

BEN HODGES

"We wanted him where they could keep an eye on him"

Dodge City, Kansas, was a boomtown and held endless amusements for cowboys eager to spend their wages after months on the trail. Two of its most famous lawmen were Bat Masterson and Wyatt Earp. One cowboy who stayed in Dodge City was Ben Hodges, the son of a black man and a Mexican woman. Hodges became notorious due to a series of ambitious swindles, none entirely successful. Soon after he arrived in Kansas, he learned of a piece of land available through a Spanish land grant and made a case for his ownership on the tenuous grounds that he was descended from old Spanish stock. He didn't get the land, but he *did* get a taste for the con game.

Hodges was able to convince railroad officials, lawyers, and bankers that he owned cattle or land, and he once applied for a job as the Dodge City livestock inspector, though much of his knowledge of cattle came from rustling. When he died in 1929, he was buried in the local cemetery, Boot Hill, near the graves of prominent cattlemen. "We wanted him where they could keep an eye on him," explained one pallbearer.

CRIMINALS AND LAWMEN

The West had a reputation for lawlessness, but Indian Territory, which is now Oklahoma, posed special problems for law enforcement. The Cherokee, Chickasaw, Choctaw, Creek, and Seminole populations formed their own governments after they were forcibly moved there before the Civil War by the U.S. government. But after the war, compensation from the United States stopped, and the tribal governments weren't able to enforce the law. Gradually, the Territory became a magnet for outlaws of every race.

CRAWFORD GOLDSBY

Even his mother referred to him as Cherokee Bill

One notorious criminal in the Territory was Crawford Goldsby, known as Cherokee Bill. His parentage was mixed: black, white, Cherokee, and possibly Sioux or Mexican. But Goldsby seems to have identified with the Indian part of his heritage, and even his mother referred to him as Cherokee Bill.

Working on his own or with a gang, Cherokee Bill robbed stagecoaches, banks, stores, and trains, and killed at least six people. He was captured after a girlfriend was used to lure him to the home of a black marshal. While awaiting execution for murder, he attempted a jailbreak, killing a guard. Brought before Isaac Parker, the famous "hanging judge" of Fort Smith, Arkansas, he was convicted again and executed on March 17, 1896, at the age of twenty.

THE RUFUS BUCK GANG

True outlaws

The Rufus Buck Gang was one of the deadliest in Indian Territory, robbing ranches, stores, and individuals. In a few days in 1895, the gang went on a crime spree that included robbery, horse theft, murder, and rape.

Rufus Buck has been described as a mix of various races; the other members were Creek and a mixed-blood Creek and Native American. Word about the gang spread quickly through the Territory, and they were captured by a posse of over one hundred men. More than seven hundred people awaited their arrival at the train station in Fort Smith where Judge Isaac Parker presided over their trial. They were convicted and hanged in July 1896.

BASS REAVES

He preached to the shackled criminals after he'd arrested them

Bass Reaves was one of a number of black marshals hired by Judge Parker, who realized he needed deputies who knew the Territory and would be trusted by the people who lived there. A former Texas slave, Reaves was tall, well built, and spoke several Indian languages, though he never learned to read. To serve an arrest warrant, he relied on his memory and, sometimes, on the criminal's own ability to read the warrant.

Reaves, like other marshals, would ride into the Territory looking for several criminals at one time. Hostile citizens, foul weather, and the fugitives themselves made the trips hazardous. But Reaves was ingenious and skillful at disguise. Once, he even pretended to be an outlaw to gain the sympathy of a criminal's mother. She revealed her son's hiding place, enabling Reaves to capture the man and his accomplice—and collect the $5,000 reward for their arrest.

As deputy marshal, Reaves had the power to arrest all lawbreakers, but he preferred to concentrate on African Americans and Indians. People said he was incorruptible: he preached to the shackled criminals after he'd arrested them. And in a well-known episode, Reaves arrested his own son after the younger man had killed his wife. At the trial, Reaves's son was convicted and sentenced to life imprisonment. Bass Reaves served as a deputy marshal for over thirty years, and as a police officer after Oklahoma became a state in 1907. He died in 1910.

BASS REAVES, a black sheriff WHO SERVED the court of Judge PARKER at Fort Smith

THE STAGECOACH DRIVER

Transportation in the Far West became critical during the gold rush, when the miners and other settlers needed shipments of goods and mail from the Eastern United States. Even after the first transcontinental railroad was completed in 1869, stagecoaches played a vital role in carrying people and supplies throughout the West. Though African Americans were important in many areas of Western transportation, from the canoes of the fur trade to railroad Pullman cars, they were rare among stage drivers, who might need to exercise authority over white passengers.

GEORGE MONROE

An exceptional stagecoach driver

George Monroe was a native of Georgia and moved with his family to California during the early years of the gold rush. He showed talent for working with horses and found employment as a stage driver in 1868, at the age of twenty-four.

Stagecoach travel could be dangerous and even life-threatening, but no passenger of George Monroe's was ever injured in his nearly twenty years of driving. His passengers included Ulysses S. Grant, President and Mrs. Rutherford B. Hayes, and General William Tecumseh Sherman. Monroe's career—and life—ended abruptly in 1886 after he was thrown by a mule. When the horses of the coach he'd been driving felt another driver's hands at the reins, they refused to budge, so Monroe, though mortally wounded, talked to the team until they were calm enough to be driven again.

GEORGE MONROE SON OF AN EARLY BLACK GOLD MINER, BECAME ONE OF CALIFORNIA'S MOST FAMOUS STAGE DRIVERS IN 1879 MONROE WAS CHOSE TO DRIVE PRESIDENT U.S. GRANT

THE WOMEN

Except among the Native Americans, women—especially African Americans—were scarce on the frontier. Some black women came west as slaves and were freed; others were homesteaders. Some became cooks in mining towns or ran rooming houses. Still others came as teachers, missionaries, even mail-order brides. Most were domestics, laundresses, seamstresses, or nurse-midwives, who learned that, in frontier areas, men would pay—and pay well—for work that women had always done. Like black men, African American women found discrimination in the West, but also higher pay and more opportunities than elsewhere in the country.

BIDDY MASON

A slave who became a woman of property

Biddy Mason won a famous court case in California, a free state that allowed slaves to pass through it in transit to another state. Biddy Mason's owner had brought her and several other slaves there from Mississippi, and in 1855 decided to move on with them to Texas. A petition was filed with the Los Angeles courts on behalf of Biddy and another woman: they wanted their freedom and wanted to stay in California with their twelve children and grandchildren. Four of the children were free, having been born in California, and a judge ruled that both women and all twelve children could stay.

As a free woman, Biddy worked as a domestic and a nurse. She saved her nurse's salary of $2.50 a week until she could buy two empty lots, and then two more. By the century's end, her estate was worth $300,000. She turned her home into a refuge for travelers and donated her money to educational causes and her church.

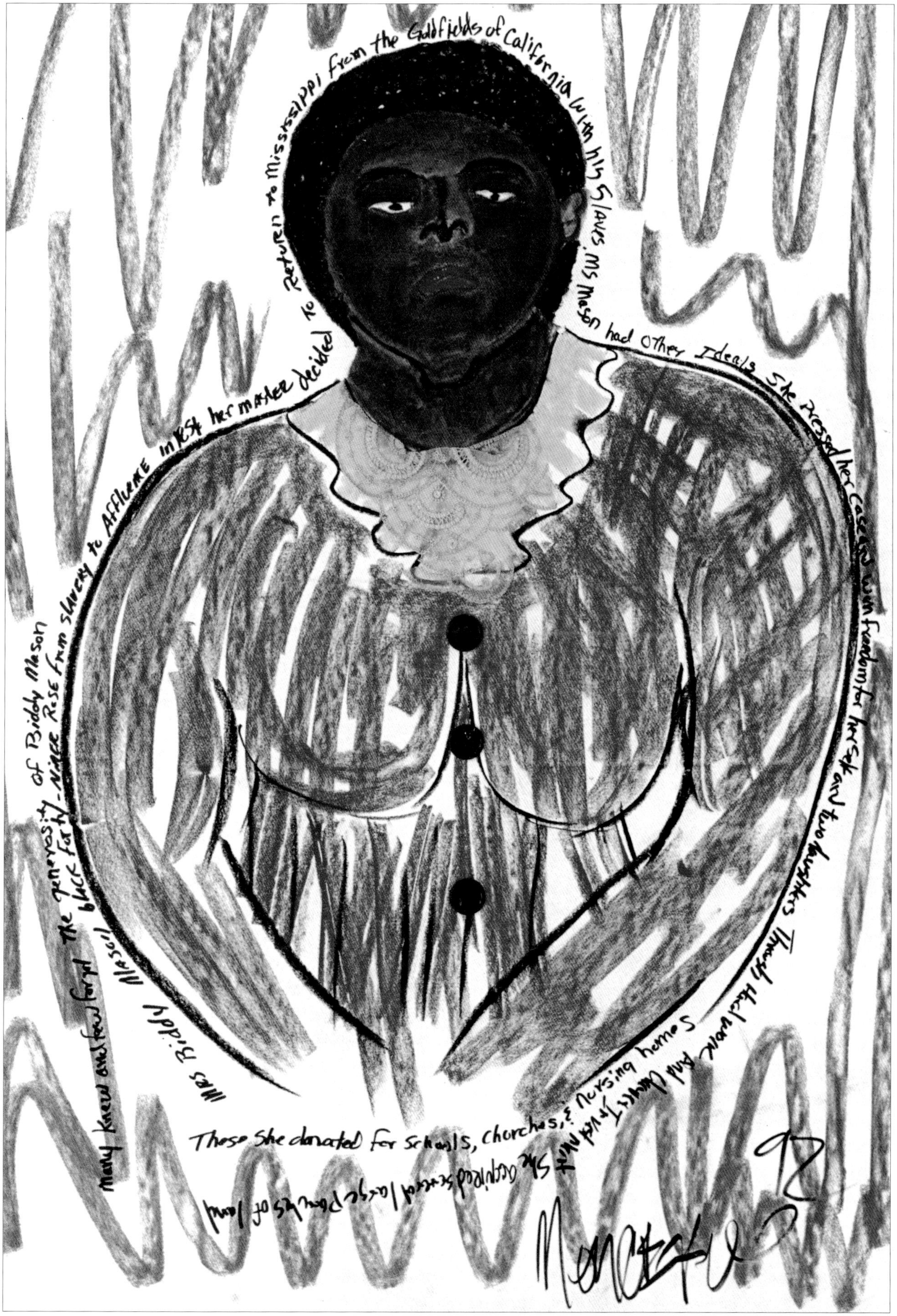

Mrs Biddy Mason! black forty-niner Rose from slavery to Affluence in 1854 her master decided to Return to Mississippi from the Goldfields of California with his slaves. Ms Mason had Other Ideals She Pressed her case and won freedom for herself and two daughters Through hard work and clever investment She acquired several large parcels of land Those she donated for schools, churches, & Nursing homes

Many knew and few forgot the generosity of Biddy Mason

CLARA BROWN

She made and lost a fortune

Clara Brown was a former slave who helped create a community. Newly freed and in her fifties, Brown cooked for a party of gold seekers traveling west to Colorado. There she established a laundry, washing shirts for fifty cents apiece. In one year, she had saved a thousand dollars to buy the freedom of her husband and children back in Kentucky. When she couldn't locate them, she brought other slaves to Colorado.

Several years later, Brown owned property in five towns. She never found her family, but she started an organization to bring blacks to the West after the Civil War. Clara Brown helped establish a church and, like Biddy Mason, was known for her good works, but unlike Mason, she was unlucky financially and died in poverty.

MARY FIELDS

She wouldn't refuse anyone a meal

A former slave whose good deeds were coupled with legendary eccentricity was Mary Fields, sometimes known as Stagecoach Mary. Fields was born in Tennessee and moved as an adult to Ohio, where she worked in a convent and then followed one of the nuns to Montana. There, she worked at a mission school for Indians; later she ran a restaurant and was a mail carrier.

Tall and heavyset, Fields dressed in men's clothing, carried a gun, and drank heavily. She could be tough, but her restaurant failed because she wouldn't refuse anyone a meal. In her old age, she was mascot to a baseball team, and the schools in her town of Cascade, Montana, closed not once but, inexplicably, *twice* a year in honor of her birthday.

Many black women in the West were nearly anonymous, and little is known about their lives beyond a photograph or a letter. But like so many others of their time, whatever their race, they hoped to find a safe home and a place for their children to grow up and be educated.

Elvira Conley, owner of a laundry in Kansas

Luticcia Parsons Butler, a nurse with the buffalo soldiers

Cathy Williams disguised herself as a man, changed her name to Williams Cathy, and served in the 9th Cavalry

A mail-order bride

BUFFALO SOLDIERS

Black soldiers served in the Revolutionary War, the War of 1812, and on both sides of the Civil War. In 1866, to protect the Western frontier, Congress passed an act giving the U.S. Army twelve new regiments, including six to be composed of African Americans. Later, the six were combined into four.

The 9th and 10th Cavalries and the 24th and 25th Infantries, often called the "brunettes" or the "buffalo soldiers," served in some of the most bitter Indian wars in the West. In many ways their lives were similar to those of white enlisted men, with the added benefit that the chaplain of each black regiment was expected to provide the recruits with an education. But the buffalo soldiers often received inferior supplies, and some of their white officers resented being posted to them. Still, the black regiments had the lowest desertion rates in the Army. On the military posts, as on the cattle drives, black and white soldiers were forced to cooperate, often developing tolerance and even respect for one another, if not true integration.

MOSES WILLIAMS

Cited for his "coolness, bravery, and unflinching devotion to duty"

During the Indian wars on the Western frontier, eleven members of the 9th Cavalry were among the eighteen black enlisted men who received the Congressional Medal of Honor. One of them was First Sergeant Moses Williams, a Pennsylvanian cited for his "coolness, bravery, and unflinching devotion to duty" as he "rallied a detachment, skillfully conducted a running fight of three or four hours, and...saved the lives of at least three of his comrades."

Moses Williams showed his heroism toward the end of a bitter and extended battle with the Apache in the Arizona and New Mexico territories. In 1876 the 9th Cavalry was dispatched to stop raiding parties led by the Apache leaders Geronimo and Juh. The Apache claimed they had been issued inferior meat and therefore needed to hunt off the reservation. Five years later, the 9th Cavalry was still fighting the Apache. In 1881, a 9th Cavalry detachment, which included Moses Williams, faced the Apache leader Nana and a party of forty in a battle lasting several hours. At one point, Williams and two other soldiers saved the lives of four men who had been cut off from the main army. By the end of 1881, the main Apache force had been subdued, and most of the 9th Cavalry had been reassigned to other duties.

THE Ninth Regiment Cavalry United States Colored Troops was organized in New Orleans in 1866 under Colonel Edward Hatch. It became a tough hard hitting unit under the fifteen year command of Major Albert P. Morrow. The Ninth served in Texas, New Mexico, Kansas, Oklahoma, Nebraska, Utah & Montana

Moses Williams Sergeant in the Ninth Cavalry

The Ninth marches out with splendid cheer. The Badlands to explore. With Colonel Hatch at their head, they never fear the foe

Williams Rallied a detachment skillfully conducted a running fight of three or four hours & by his coolness, bravery & unflinching devotion to duty in standing by his commanding officer in an exposed position under fire from a large party of Indians saved the lives of at least three of his comrades

Soon they rode from Christmas eve till dawn of Christmas day. The Redskins heard the Ninth was near and fled in great dismay.

RECEIVED THE MEDAL OF HONOR IN 1881

Outina, a sixteenth-century Timucuan chief in Florida

NATIVE AMERICANS

At the same time that African Americans were finding new freedom in the West, various Native American peoples were trapped in the final stages of conflicts that had begun centuries earlier. From the first, settlers from Europe, where land was owned by individuals, had been puzzled by the view held by many Native Americans that the land was there for them to use, not to own. And as explorers from England, Spain, France, and other countries fanned out across the North American continent, they became more and more excited by possibility—here was land, apparently unclaimed, to be settled and exploited for profit.

And the newcomers did settle. By the mid-nineteenth century, the Native American populations had been reduced drastically through disease and warfare, and had come to occupy ever smaller portions of what was now the United States. In a familiar and always tragic pattern, as settlers spread into new territories, the government would negotiate with the local Indians, who were not United States citizens but separate nations, and would trade a specified amount of money—and sometimes other support such as food rations—for land. The Indians would have to agree to occupy different land, frequently a reservation, often an area already occupied by other Indian peoples, who were sometimes enemies. The Indian Removal Act of 1830 allowed the government to move most of the Native peoples out of the Eastern United States.

The results were predictable and catastrophic for the Indians. As more and more of the country was settled, those Native Americans who were still at large became more skilled at dealing with the government, and more desperate in their efforts to keep their own land. The Native American leaders who led these final battles in the West became famous as warriors and as articulate, canny diplomats, sometimes more respected in the larger culture than their white opponents. In their defeat, they became legends.

JOHN HORSE

"This is a Negro, not an Indian war; and if not put down, the south will feel the effects of it on their slave population."

—General Thomas Jesup, 1836

Of all the Southeastern tribes, the Seminole fought hardest against removal. Their numbers included many African Americans—runaways as well as slaves purchased from the Spanish. Cultivating their own farms on Seminole land, these slaves were forced to give produce to their owners, but otherwise had far greater freedom than most other slaves. They were influential interpreters of white customs and language, and often intermarried with the tribe.

The relative freedom of black Seminole represented a threat to white slaveowners and influenced the government removal policy. The removal of the Seminole from Florida cost the United States government over $20 million, the most expensive of the Indian wars. Once resettled, the Seminole lived uneasily in Indian Territory among the Creek, whose own black slaves had far less freedom.

In 1850, a delegation of two hundred Seminole appeared on the Mexican border and asked to be admitted as settlers. Led by a chief called Coacoochee, or Wild Cat, together with a mixed-blood Negro Seminole named John Horse, they took up farming and aided the Mexican government by patrolling for raiders and other, hostile Indians. Much later, in the 1870s, the Seminole would serve *with* the United States Army, including the black regiments, as scouts in the Western Indian wars.

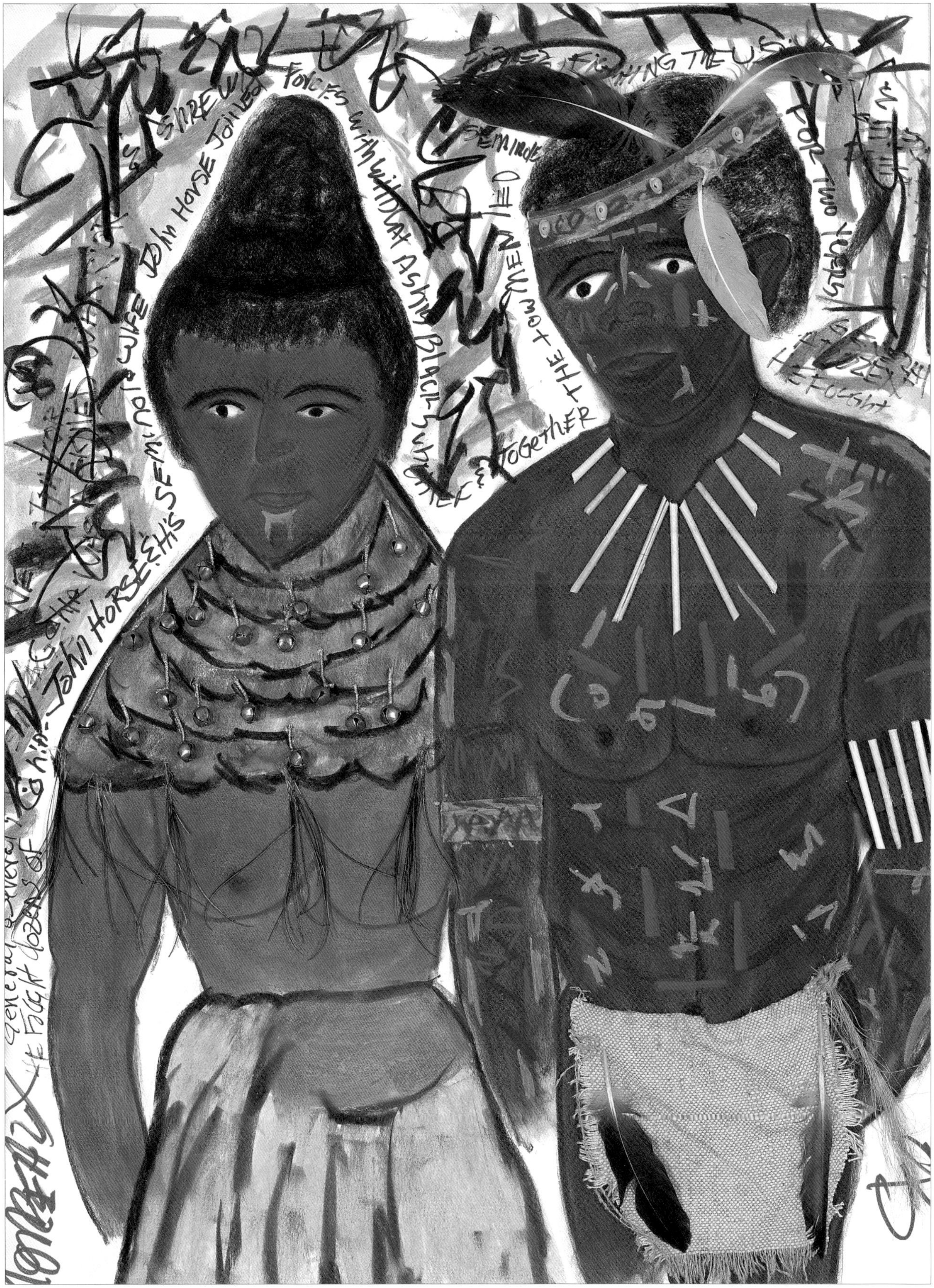

The white man has taken our country killed all of our game was not satisfied with that, but killed our wives & children now no peace. We want to go & meet our families in the spirit land. We loved the whites until we found out they lied to us & robbed us of all we had. We have raised the battle ax until death.

LITTLE RAVEN Chief of the ARAPAHO

LITTLE RAVEN

An Indian leader who met with the Governor of Colorado to forestall further warfare

The Pikes Peak gold rush attracted 100,000 men to the Colorado territory in 1859, overwhelming the native Cheyenne and Arapaho. As often happened, the sheer mass of settlers forced the government's hand, and the Senate authorized negotiations with the local tribes to sign a treaty that would set aside land for a reservation for them. Unfortunately, the land chosen for the reservation was inferior, and only a few chiefs signed.

The uneasy peace ended in 1864, when war broke out between the Indians and the settlers. With the Civil War draining U.S. Army resources, volunteer militia led the fight against the Indians. Little Raven, an Arapaho, and Black Kettle, a Cheyenne chief, were among the Indian leaders who met with the Governor of Colorado and the territory's military commander, Colonel John M. Chivington, to forestall further warfare. But in November 1864, Chivington attacked Black Kettle's village at Sand Creek, killing two hundred Cheyenne, including women and children. Little Raven, camped nearby, escaped.

The Indians soon struck back, as Lakota, Comanche, Kiowa, and other Plains Indians, as well as the Cheyenne and Arapaho, attacked the settlers and wagon trains that traveled across their lands. The Civil War was ending, but a continued military presence in the West seemed inevitable.

ELY PARKER

A lawyer who couldn't argue a case in court because he was an Indian

As Commissioner of Indian Affairs, Ely Parker was at the center of President Grant's peace policy. A Seneca chief from New York, Parker had negotiated for his own tribe's land while still a teenager. He was trained as a lawyer and an engineer, but he was not allowed to argue a case in court because he was an Indian and therefore not a citizen.

But by 1868 few would have challenged Parker's abilities—or even his citizenship. As General Grant's aide-de-camp, Parker had written out the terms of General Robert E. Lee's surrender at Appomattox. He had discussed Indian affairs more than once with President Lincoln, including at a meeting on the last day of the President's life. His office employed seventy agents, who reported to fifteen supervisors. Parker saw their job as preparing Indians to "submit to the inevitable change in their mode of life and pursuits more congenial to a civilized state."

As an Indian who had succeeded brilliantly in the white world, Parker saw no reason why others couldn't do the same. But the situation in the West was far more complicated, because Indians hunted and fished on land that others saw as potential mines, ranches, and farms.

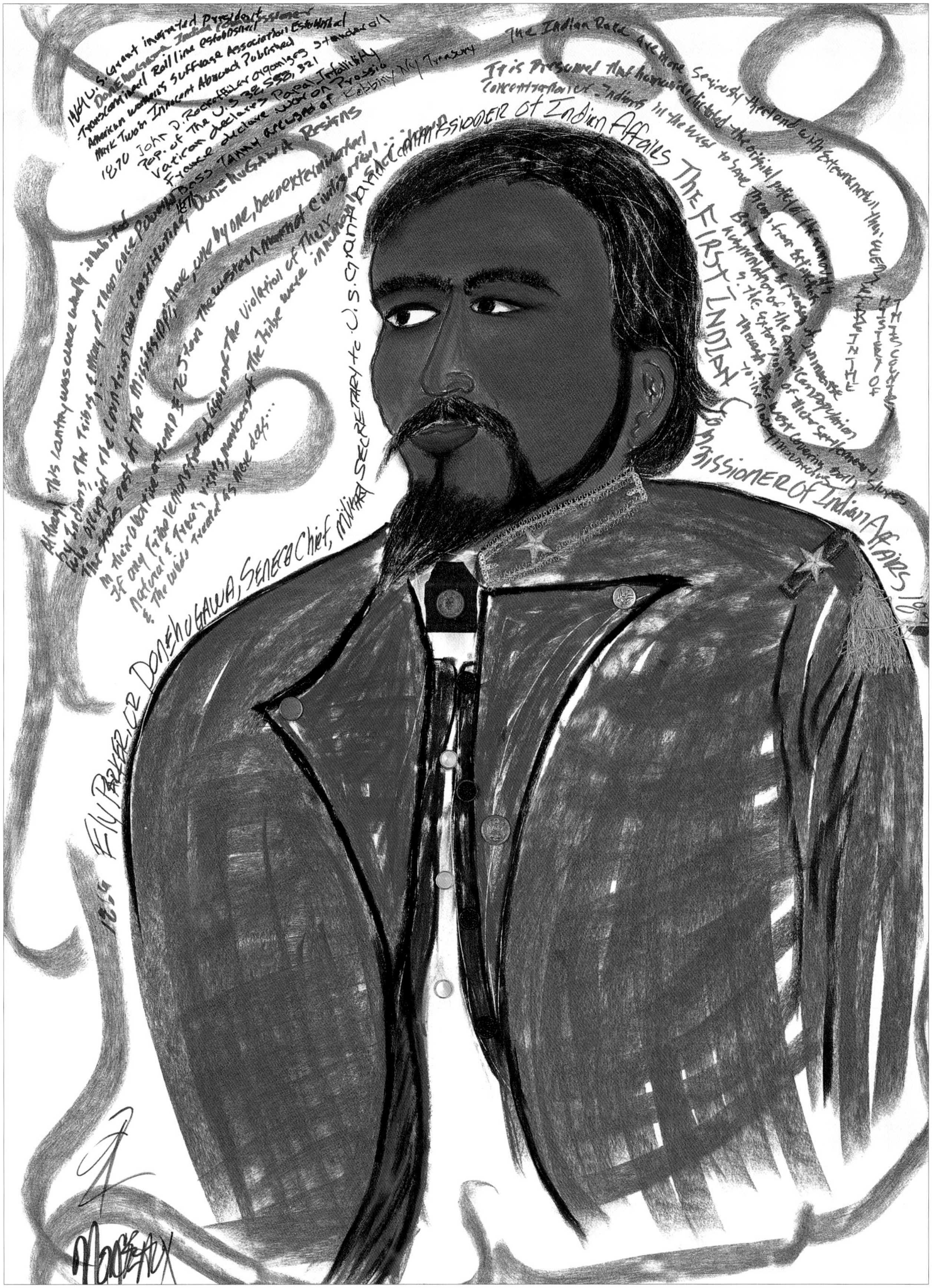
ELY PARKER, OR DONEHOGAWA, SENECA Chief, military SECRETARY to U.S. GRANT
COMMISSIONER of Indian Affairs
THE FIRST INDIAN COMMISSIONER OF Indian AFFAIRS

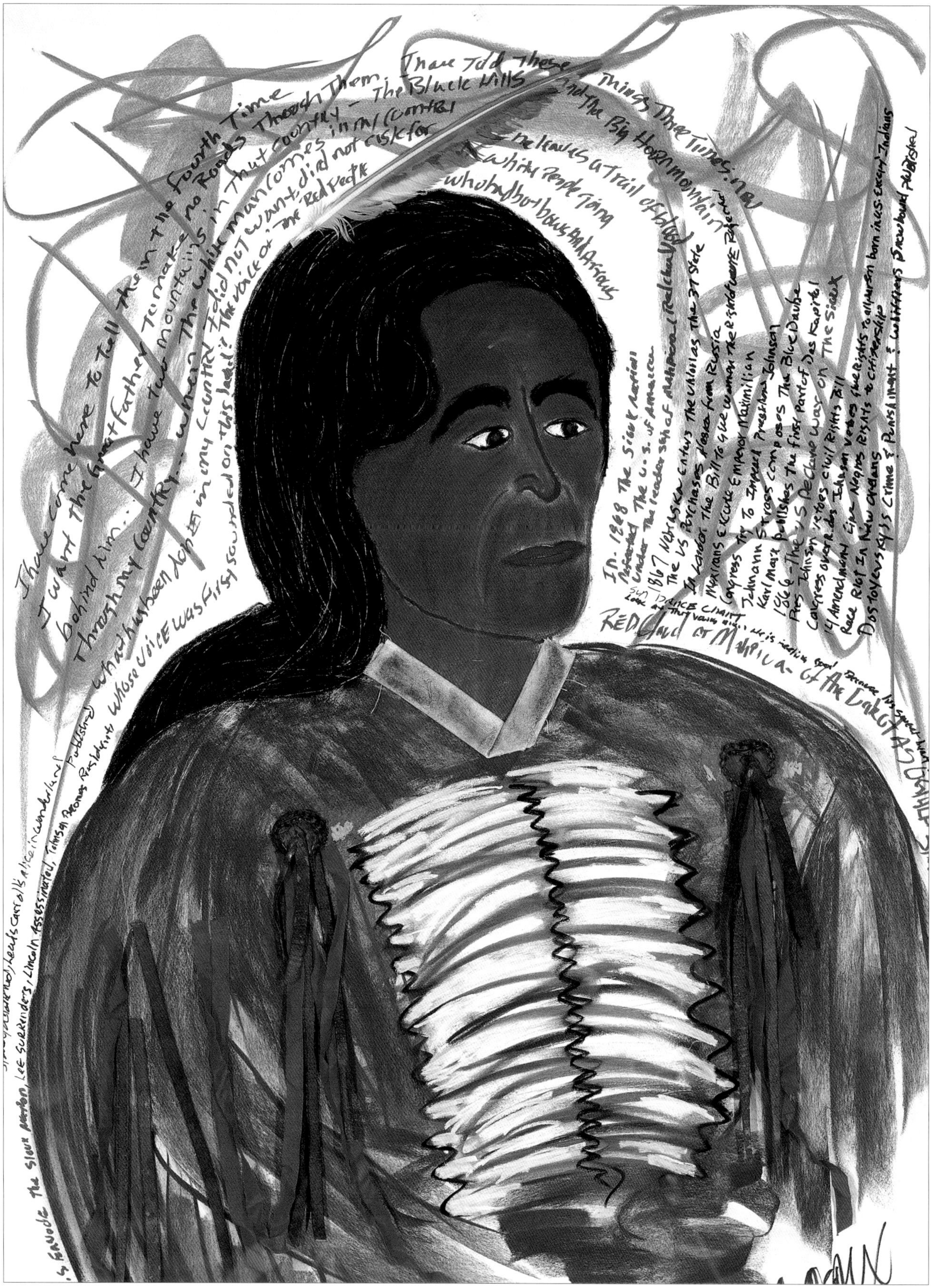
I have come here to tell them the fourth time
I want the Great Father to make no Roads through them
behind him. I have two mountains in that country - The Black Hills
through my country ... where the white man comes in my countr
what has been done in my country I did not want did not ask for
whose voice was first sounded on this land! The voice of the Red People
I have told these things three times
And the Big Horn Mountains
He leaves a Trail of Blood
white People going
RED Cloud

RED CLOUD

"The white children have surrounded me and left me nothing but an island"

The Lakota chief Red Cloud had proven himself in war against the Crow, Pawnee, Ute, and Shoshone. By 1866 he was a powerful warrior, and the government knew it. One problem the United States government had in negotiating with Indians was knowing who might have the power to sign a treaty. Leadership even within a single tribe was complicated, and the government wished in vain for one leader who could speak for all. For a time, Red Cloud seemed to be that chief.

But that year, negotiations to move the Lakota bands to a reservation broke off at Fort Laramie, Wyoming, when Red Cloud accused the government of treating the chiefs like children and forcing them onto ever smaller patches of land. He promised the combined tribes would fight for their last hunting ground.

In 1866, Red Cloud and other Indians harassed parties of would-be miners on the new Bozeman Trail in Montana, laying siege to Army forts along the trail. And in August 1868, he personally led an attack against soldiers guarding a woodcutting operation near Fort Kearney. Soon after, a new treaty was offered the Lakota, providing a reservation that covered all of present-day South Dakota west of the Missouri River. At least three-fourths of the adult male Indians referred to in the treaty had to ratify it. Red Cloud held out, not signing until the government agreed to abandon its forts along the Bozeman Trail and close the trail to whites. It was the only time an Indian would win a war against the United States.

SITTING BULL

"A hard time I have"

While some Indians moved onto the reservations, other bands stayed fiercely independent. As they became more aware of the threat to their way of life, some Lakota chiefs designated Sitting Bull the leader of the non-reservation Indians. By the mid-1870s, Sitting Bull saw the threat extending to the Black Hills, land the Lakota prized highest of all. The hills were becoming overrun by gold prospectors, and the United States government, powerless to stop them, decided instead to force the remaining Lakota from this territory.

In early 1877, U.S. soldiers were spotted in the Lakota territory. When the tribes gathered for their annual sun dance in June, Sitting Bull described a vision in which he had seen many soldiers and horses falling upside down into an Indian village. They were attacking the village, but they would be killed, along with some Indians. The Indians were not to scalp or mutilate their bodies. It would be a great victory.

A few weeks later, Sitting Bull's vision came true with the battle of Little Bighorn. The disastrous invasion by Lieutenant Colonel George Custer—"Long Hair" to the Indians—became known as the finest Indian triumph and the United States Army's most stinging defeat. Sitting Bull and Crazy Horse, another chief, became world famous for their leadership in defense of their homes and families. The battle also proved to be the downfall of the non-reservation Indian bands, for the Army then devoted every resource to subduing them. Sitting Bull took pride in being the last to surrender, retreating to Canada until 1881, when he surrendered in Fort Buford, North Dakota. Soon after, he composed a song:

A warrior
I have been
Now
It is all over
A hard time
I have.

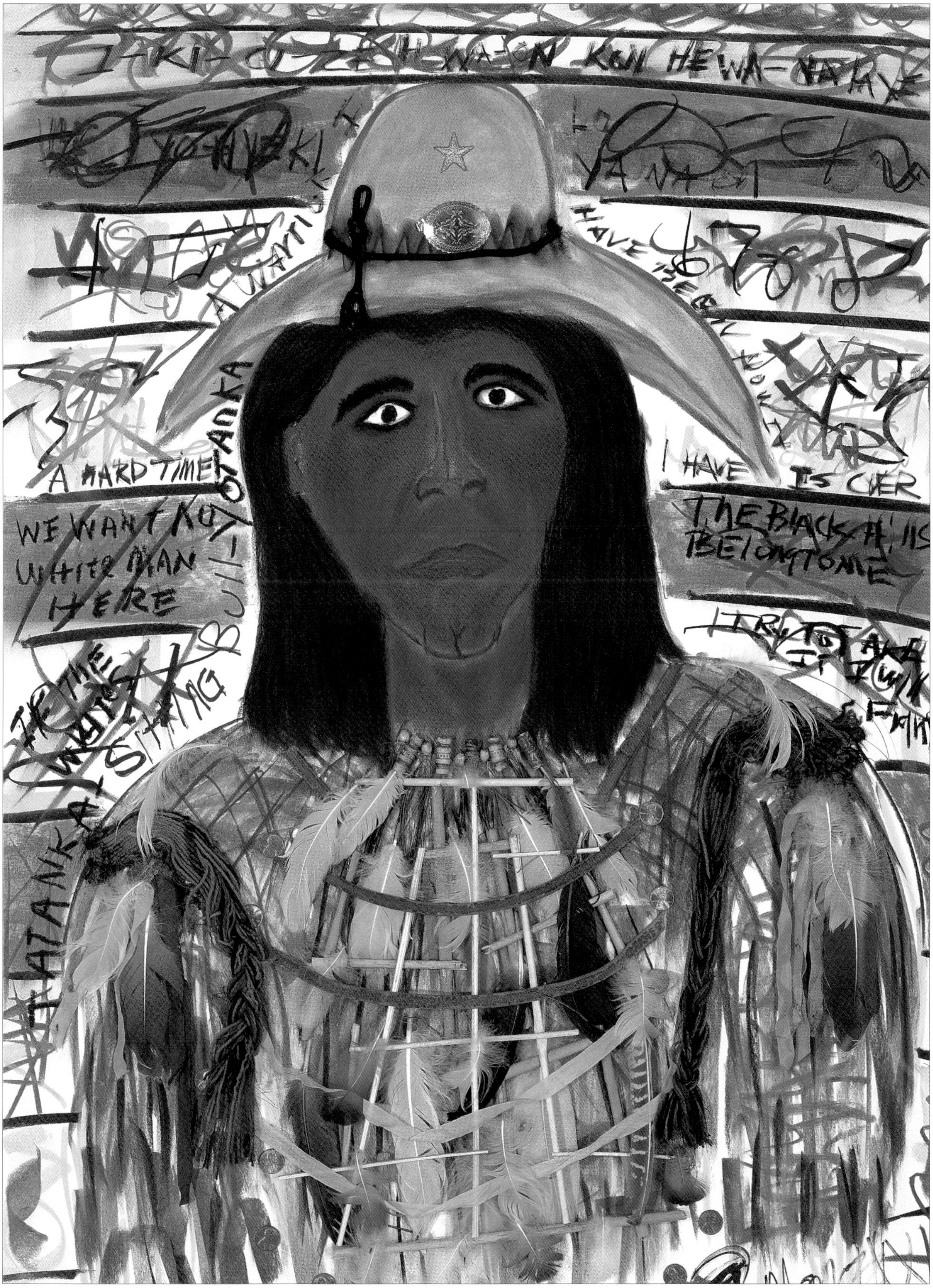

A HARD TIME
WE WANT NO WHITE MAN HERE
I HAVE
IS OVER
THE BLACK HILLS BELONG TO ME

STANDING BEAR

He found Indian Territory unsuitable for working or living

The Ponca were a small tribe that had been resettled in Indian Territory after their land, in South Dakota, had been appropriated for a Lakota reservation. There were fewer than seven hundred Ponca when they were driven from their homes in 1877. Their numbers shrank quickly through illness. In 1879, one chief, Standing Bear, had had enough. His grandson had just died, and he decided to bury him in the tribe's true home in the Dakotas. With a small band of Ponca, Standing Bear started the journey home, but in Omaha they were arrested and jailed.

The world was changing, and more people were aware that Indians were being treated unfairly. Standing Bear's plight caught the interest of an Omaha newspaperman and former abolitionist, Thomas Henry Tibbles, who hired legal counsel and arranged for the case to be tried in court. Suddenly the whole nation knew what this trial meant: was an Indian entitled to the legal protection due any other person living within the United States? If so, Standing Bear couldn't be forced to move or live anywhere against his will.

The case was tried in April 1879. Standing Bear testified that he wanted to work on the land, and he found Indian Territory unsuitable for working or living. He wanted to go to his own land, to bury his grandson there, and to live there the rest of his life.

On May 12, Judge Elmer Dundy filed his decision, stating that the "individual Indian possesses the clear and God-given right to withdraw from his tribe and forever live away from it." Furthermore, no authority justified the Commissioner of Indian Affairs "to remove any Indian by force to any place." Under the decision, Standing Bear—like any other Indian—was a person by the terms of the Fourteenth Amendment. Standing Bear was free to go, and he did, settling on the Dakota reservation where he had lived before 1877.

KINTPUASH

Executed for murder

The Modoc were a small California tribe; in 1864 they had signed a treaty and given up their land in exchange for space on a reservation in Oregon. Just a year later, Kintpuash, a Modoc leader known by the whites as Captain Jack, led a number of homesick families back to settle along the Lost River south of the California-Oregon border.

For several years tensions built as more white settlers moved onto the land now occupied by Kintpuash. In 1872 the Army was called in to force the Modoc to return to the reservation. Kintpuash and sixty of his men defended the tribe for four months, evading the Army on the inhospitable lava beds that formed the southern shore of Tule Lake. Finally a peace commission was called. The negotiations splintered the Modoc, and Kintpuash reluctantly agreed to a plot to kill the peace commissioners. On April 11, 1873, he joined an attack that left two members of the delegation dead, including a U.S. Army general.

As Kintpuash had feared, this attack brought more soldiers to the area, and the Modoc were forced to surrender. Captain Jack, along with three others, was executed for murder; the few remaining members of his band were banished to Indian Territory.

CHIEF KINTPUASH (CAPTAIN JACK) OF THE MODOCS

CHIEF Joseph of the Nez Perces

HIN-MAH-TOO-YAH-LAT-KEKHT (CHIEF JOSEPH)

"I would have given my own life if I could have undone the killing of white men by my people. I blame my own men and I blame the white men"

One tribe that had seemed immune to the troubles of many Western Indians was the Nez Perce, who lived near where the present-day states of Idaho, Washington, and Oregon meet. Their first contact with whites had been the Lewis and Clark expedition in 1805. The travelers traded some of the valuable goods they carried for food—fish and roots. William Clark wrote that these Indians "appeared disposed to give us every assistance in their power during our distress." They were, he also noted, "stout likely men, handsom women, and verry dressy in their way..."

Seventy years later, the Nez Perce were prosperous and had adapted well to the influx from the East, first fur traders, then settlers. They were a trading and traveling people, the only Indians to practice selective breeding of horses. Many had converted to Christianity and had friendly relations with white settlers; no Nez Perce had ever killed a white man or woman.

But the population of settlers and gold miners was exploding. In 1855, a large reservation had been created for the Nez Perce in present-day southern Idaho; commissioners were sent in 1863 to negotiate a treaty for a smaller reservation. As whites poured into their lands, those chiefs who hadn't signed the new treaty saw the threat. The government, too, realized it couldn't contain the white intruders. Instead, it would have to find a way to move the remaining Nez Perce onto a reservation.

In 1876, one chief, Hin-mah-too-yah-lat-kekht, known to the whites as Joseph, explained to government representatives why his people weren't bound by the 1863 treaty: "Suppose a white man should come to me and say, 'Joseph, I like your horses, and I want to buy them.' I say to him, 'No, my horses suit me, I will not sell them.' Then he goes to my neighbor and says to him, 'Joseph has some good horses. I want to buy them but he refuses to sell.' My neighbor answers, 'Pay me the money, and I will sell you Joseph's horses.' The white man returns to me and says, 'Joseph, I have bought your horses and you must let me have them.' If we sold our lands to the government, this is the way they were bought."

In spite of this persuasive argument, the Indian Bureau decreed in May 1877 that all the Nez Perce should come onto the reservation. Faced with no alternative but war, the bands agreed. They had only a month to gather their valuable stock of horses and cattle. But in the last days before the deadline, a few young men disobeyed the chiefs and went on a rampage, killing four white men. The settlers demanded retribution, and U.S. Army troops were sent in: another Indian war had broken out. Later Joseph wrote: "I would have given my own life if I could have undone the killing of white men by my people. I blame my own men and I blame the white men."

Through the long summer of 1877, a band of 750 Nez Perce Indians fought and retreated over a 1,700-mile journey that took them from their home in Oregon's Wallowa Valley, now overrun by settlers, through Idaho, Montana, and into Yellowstone Park. Their antagonist was General Oliver Howard, a one-armed Civil War veteran. In one engagement after another, the Nez Perce held their own against an army of much greater numbers and resources.

The Nez Perce retreat was followed closely in the newspapers, and people across the country saw Chief Joseph as a hero. But as summer turned to fall, it became obvious to Joseph and the other Nez Perce that they would find no refuge on the Great Plains with the Army still on their trail. Their only hope was to reach the Canadian border, where they might join Sitting Bull in exile. In early October, as snow fell, the Nez Perce fought a final battle in Montana's Bear Paw Mountains, not far from the border. A group of slightly over two hundred Nez Perce broke away to cross the border and join Sitting Bull's group; just over four hundred stayed with Joseph.

On October 5, Joseph handed over his rifle. He told an interpreter: "Tell General Howard I know his heart. What he told me before, I have it in my heart. I am tired of fighting. Our chiefs are killed. Looking Glass is dead. Toohoolhoolzote is dead. The old men are all dead. It is the young men who say, 'yes' or 'no.' He who led the young men [his brother, Ollokot, a war chief] is dead. It is cold, and we have no blankets. The little children are freezing to death. My people, some of them, have run away to the hills, and have no blankets, no food. No one knows where they are—perhaps freezing to death. I want to have time to look for my children, and see how many of them I can find. Maybe I shall find them among the dead. Hear me, my chiefs! I am tired. My heart is sick and sad. From where the sun now stands I will fight no more forever."

The legend of Chief Joseph grew after the surrender. Even so, the Nez Perce were sent to Indian Territory. In 1882, Joseph and some of his followers were allowed to return to the Pacific Northwest, though not to their home in the Wallowa Valley. Much later, a former aide to General Howard wrote: "I think that, in his long career, Joseph cannot accuse the United States of one single act of justice."

COCHISE

"When God made the world he gave one part to the white man and another to the Apache"

Cochise's name came from the Apache word for oak; he was the most prominent Apache chief of his day. He had fought Mexicans all his life, but maintained a cautious peace with the Americans. That changed in 1861, when Cochise was invited to the tent of George Bascom, an Army lieutenant. Believing Bascom to be friendly, Cochise had brought his wife and family; he was unprepared when Bascom accused him of stealing cattle and kidnapping a local boy. Suddenly aware that soldiers were surrounding them, Cochise slashed through the tent with a knife and escaped, but his family was held hostage. In retaliation, Cochise's band ambushed a wagon train and an Army party; they killed and took hostages. And though Bascom eventually released Cochise's wife and two children, he killed the adult men among his hostages. Cochise lay low for two months, then he led a war party on weekly raids through Arizona. At first, his strategy appeared to be working, as nearly all whites, Army and civilian, left the territory with the start of the Civil War. But over the next ten years, the white population of the Southwest grew to nearly ten thousand, compared with six to eight thousand Apache. As Cochise said in 1871, "When I was young I walked all over this country, east and west, and saw no other people than the Apache. After many summers I walked again and found another race of people had come to take it. How is it?"

Finally he had to admit his people might be better off on a reservation. In 1872 he negotiated a treaty for a large reservation in southeastern Arizona. He died in 1874.

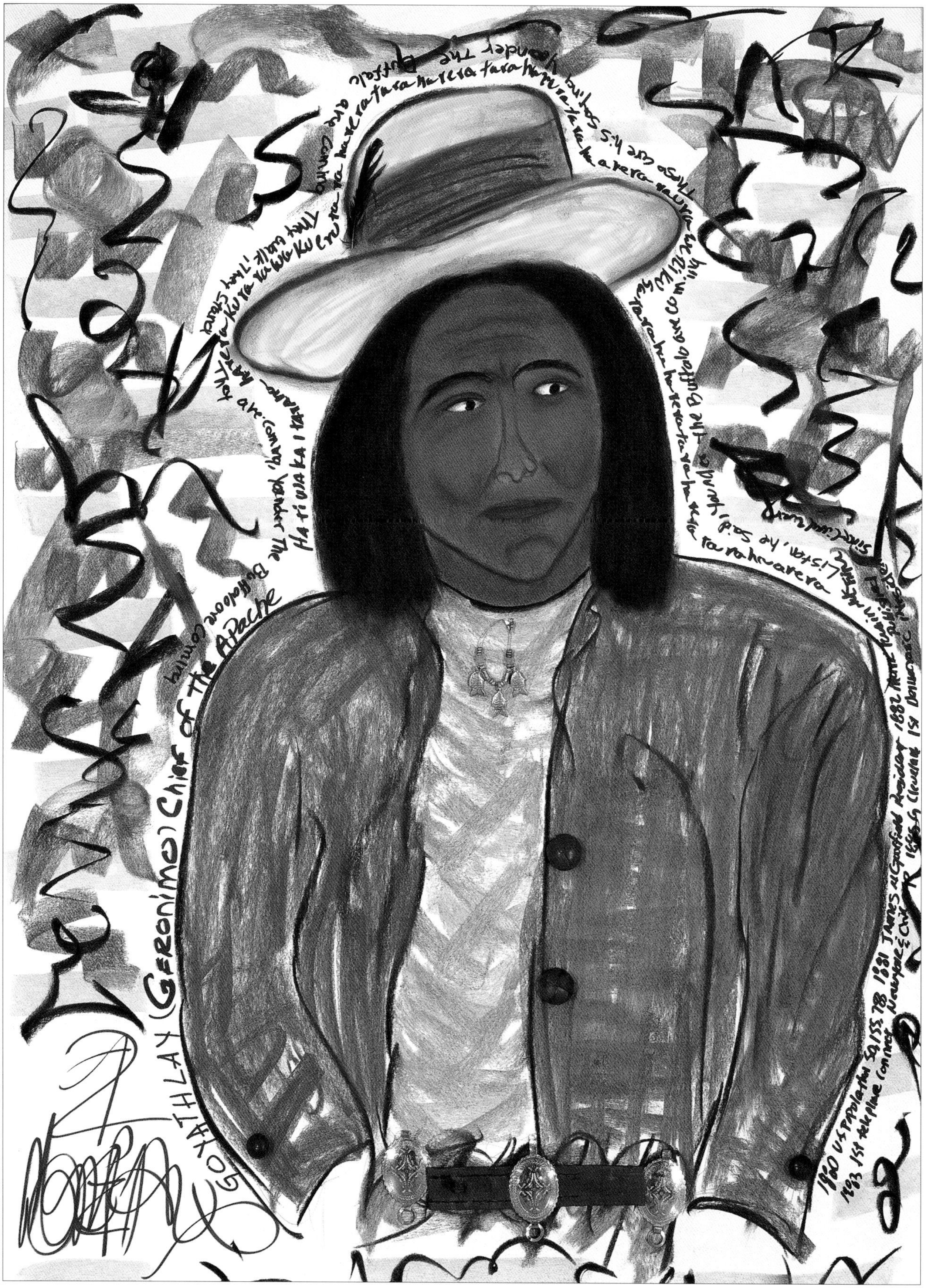
GOYATHLAY (Geronimo) Chief of the Apache

GERONIMO

"I feared treachery. . . We were reckless of our lives, because we felt that every man's hand was against us"

A member of the band that took revenge after the kidnapping of Cochise's wife and children, Geronimo knew the bitterness of attacks against family. In 1859, when he was in his early twenties, his mother, wife, and three young children were among a number of Apache women and children slain by Mexican soldiers. For all his life, Geronimo would hate Mexicans for murdering his family. A year later, in a battle for revenge, Geronimo fought as if he believed bullets could not harm him. He had had a vision that this was so. During the battle, it was the Mexicans who gave him the name Geronimo. Faced with an Apache who seemed not to care if he lived, they shouted, "¡*Cuidado* (Watch out)! Geronimo!" possibly invoking St. Jerome.

Geronimo became the leader of the free Apaches during the early 1880s, leading them in some of the most bitter battles of the Indian wars. He was secure in his location in Mexico's Sierra Madre Mountains, where neither country's army could track him. His band raided ranches, towns, and other outposts on both sides of the border. He surrendered a total of four times, living on and off reservations, but each time retreating. He wrote: "I feared treachery...We were reckless of our lives, because we felt that every man's hand was against us."

In 1886, Geronimo and a small band of fugitives surrendered for the last time. They were transported to Florida, and later were resettled in Indian Territory. Like other Indians, he never returned to his homeland, though he wrote in his autobiography: "There is no climate or soil which, to my mind, is equal to that of Arizona...It is my land, my home, my fathers' land...If I must die in bondage–I hope that the remnant of the Apache tribe may, when I am gone, be granted the one privilege which they request–to return to Arizona."

BLACK AND RED UNITED

Whether runaways, adventurers, or victims of kidnappings, members of the various races—black, white, Indian, and Mexican—sometimes chose to live among one another and to marry. Some tribes, like the Seminole, became substantially mixed, and today many Americans have mixed African American and Indian heritage.

Edmonia Lewis, known as Wildfire, had a black father and a Chippewa mother. She grew up among the Chippewa in New York, attended Oberlin College, and eventually moved to Italy, becoming a sculptor

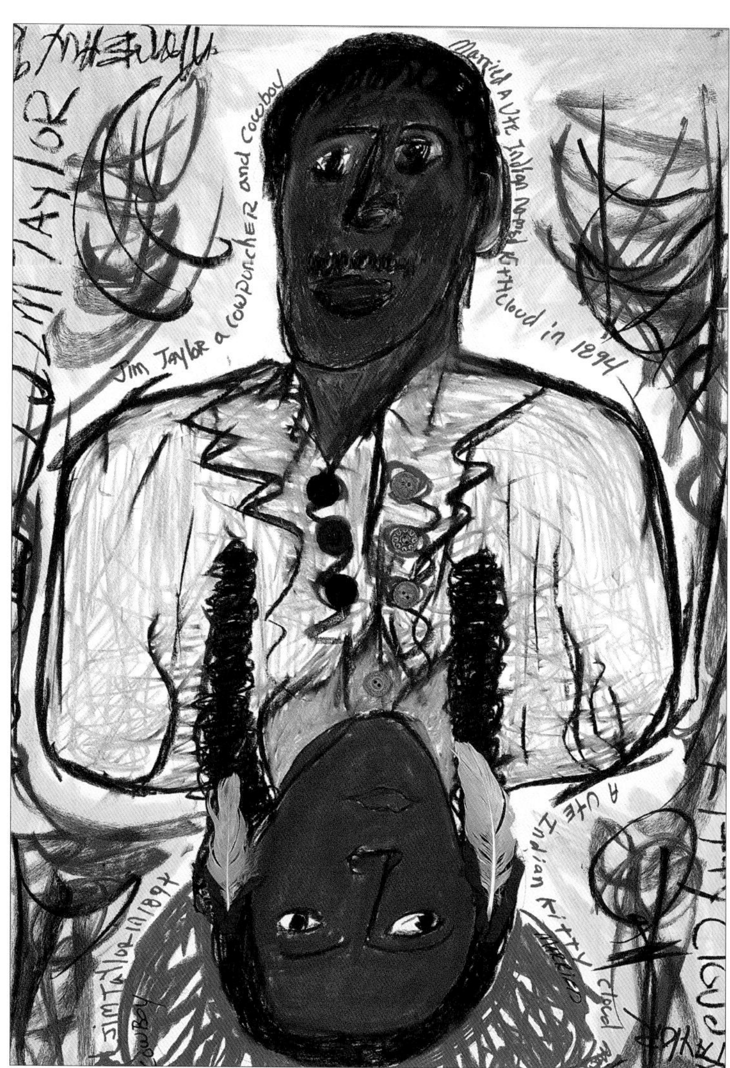

John Taylor was an African American who lived among the Ute, inhabitants of Colorado and Utah. In 1894 he married Kitty Cloud, a Ute

Diana Fletcher, also black, lived with the Kiowa on the Southwestern frontier

Juanita was the wife of Manuelita of the Navaho, who was among the last of his tribe to surrender, in 1866

THE RODEO

The roots of the rodeo lie in games played by cowboys throughout the Americas. Over time, competitions involving horseback riding, roping, and the taming of cattle became less the pastime of the working cowboy and more a form of mass entertainment that helped romanticize the legend of the Wild West.

BILL PICKETT

"A mere man, unarmed"

In 1904, *Harper's Weekly* described a cowboy carnival in Cheyenne, Wyoming: "The great event of the celebration this year was the remarkable feat of Will Pickett, a Negro hailing from Taylor, Texas…20,000 people watched with wonder and admiration a mere man, unarmed and without a device or appliance of any kind, attack a fiery, wild-eyed, and powerful steer and throw it with his teeth."

Willie (Bill) Pickett was born in Texas in 1871, the son of former slaves. He started working with cattle as a small boy. He learned that if he bit the lip of a steer, then used his weight to throw it to the ground, the animal would be quiet and could be branded.

As an adult, Bill Pickett perfected this skill in exhibitions. Bulldogging, as it was called, became a permanent rodeo event. Cowboys had always competed in their spare time, and rodeos, some with all African American performers, became a permanent part of Western culture. The rodeo made the life of a cowboy seem exciting, just as the spectacle of an aging Lakota or Apache chief in a Wild West show brought a picture of the recent past to people who would never be menaced by Indians who were fighting for their homes. For decades, this romantic version of the West would seem an embodiment of the country's spirit.

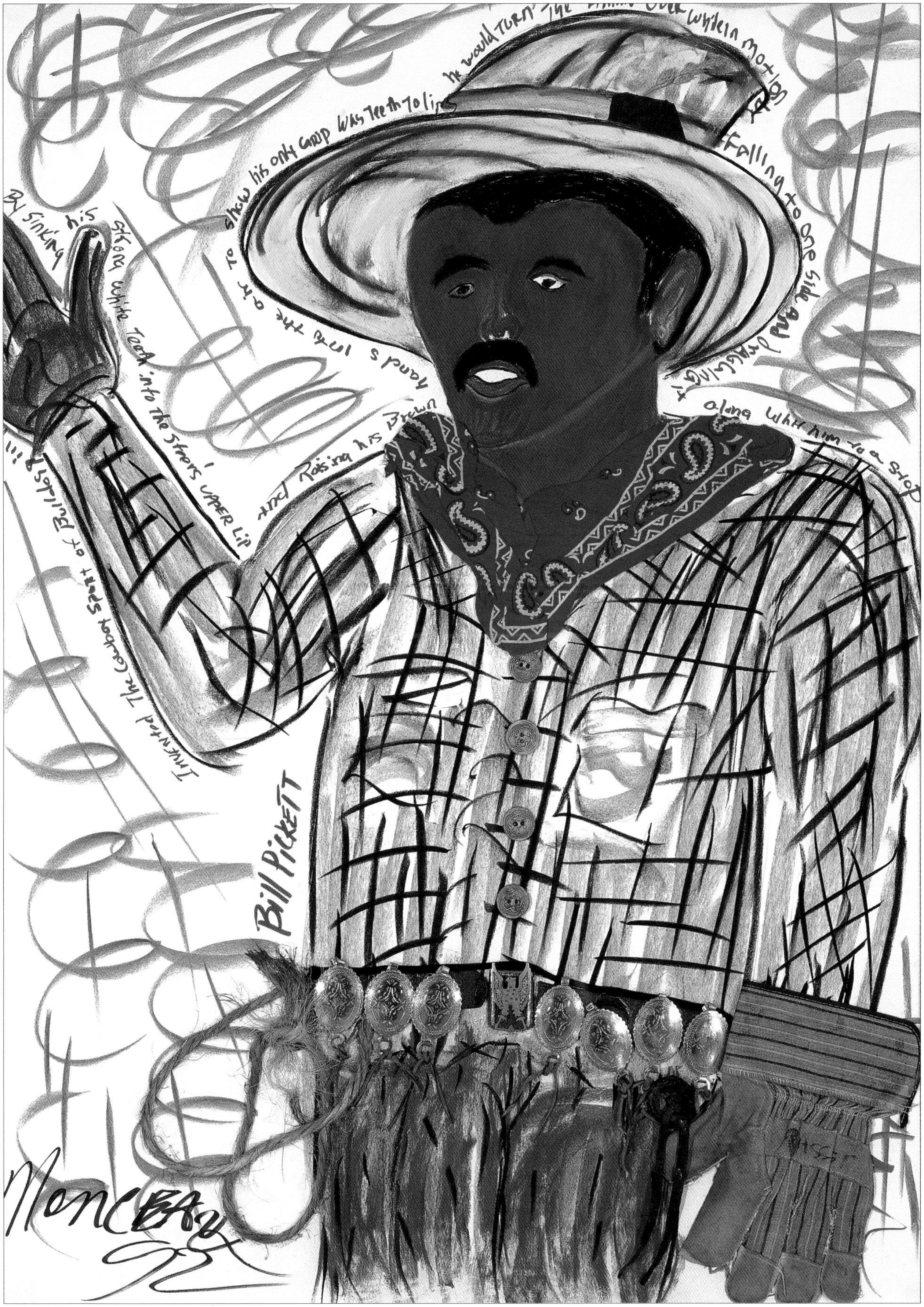
By sinking his strong white teeth into the steers upper lip
and raising his brown hands in the air to show his only grip was teeth to lips
he would turn the
while in motion
falling to one side and dragging it along with him to a stop
I invented the cowboy sport of Bulldogging!!!
Bill Pickett

A NOTE ON SOURCES AND FURTHER READING

The many sources consulted for visual references on the portraits include *500 Nations* by Alvin Josephy (Knopf, 1994), Paul W. Stewart's *Black Cowboy* (Black American West Museum and Heritage Center, 1996), and *Bury My Heart at Wounded Knee* by Dee Brown (Holt, 1971), in addition to others listed below.

Those who are interested in further reading about the West and the role of African Americans and Native Americans in the West may be faced both with too much material and with not enough. While almost no other area of American history has been covered in such detail as the West, much of the history of the black West has been, until recently, unavailable except in scholarly journals and other records. But as stories of African Americans, women, and Native Americans, and largely unknown facts about the history of all races, continue to surface, they do make their way to a general readership, often reinterpreted by each new generation.

Among many other sources consulted for background material is *The Negro Cowboys* by Philip Durham and Everett L. Jones (University of Nebraska Press, 1983). It is somewhat dated but a good starting point. The published and unpublished work of the late Kenneth W. Porter is an enormous resource culled from primary sources, now out of print but available for study at the New York Public Library's Schomburg Center for Research in Black Culture. One work by Porter has been brought up-to-date and reissued: *The Black Seminoles: History of a Freedom-Seeking People*, eds. Alcione M. Amos and Thomas P. Senter (University Press of Florida, 1996).

William Loren Katz has written several books about African Americans in the West. *Black Indians* (Atheneum, 1986) and *The Black West* (Simon & Schuster, 1987) are especially good starting points for students interested in the subject. Nat Love's autobiography, *The Life and Adventures of Nat Love* (University of Nebraska Press, 1995), is an entertaining though probably somewhat inaccurate life story of a black cowboy. William H. Leckie's *The Buffalo Soldiers: A Narrative of the Negro Cavalry in the West* (University of Oklahoma Press, 1995) is an academic history of the black cavalry regiments. Bailey C. Hanes's *Bill Pickett, Bulldogger* (University of Oklahoma Press, 1989) is a biography of one important figure. But much history of African Americans in the West still awaits publication for the general reader.

Leonard Dinnerstein's *Natives and Strangers: A Multicultural History of America* (Oxford University Press, 1996) is a good general history. David Dary's *Cowboy Culture: A Saga of Five Centuries* (University Press of Kansas, 1989), Richard W. Slatta's *Cowboys of the*

Americas (Yale University Press, 1990) and William Savage's *The Cowboy Hero* (University of Oklahoma Press, 1979) chronicle the history of the cowboy. Patricia Nelson Limerick's *The Legacy of Conquest: The Unbroken Past of the American West* (W. W. Norton, 1988) and *Under an Open Sky: Rethinking America's Western Past,* eds. William Cronon, George Miles, and Jay Gitlin (W. W. Norton, 1993) are summaries of recent scholarship of the West and more inclusive of other cultures than older works. Reginald Horsman's *Race and Manifest Destiny* (Harvard University Press, 1981) is a helpful chronicle of how historical thinking has changed on racial matters. Glenda Riley's *The Female Frontier* (University Press of Kansas, 1988) and Sandra L. Myres, *Westering Women and the Frontier Experience, 1800-1915* (University of New Mexico Press, 1982) are important histories of women in the West.

General histories of Native Americans in the West include Alvin Josephy's *The Indian Heritage of America* (Knopf, 1968) and *The Patriot Chiefs: A Chronicle of American Indian Resistance* (Viking, 1969), Robert M. Utley's *The Indian Frontier of the American West 1846-1890* (University of New Mexico Press, 1984), and *Indian Wars* by Utley and Wilcomb E. Washburn (American Heritage, 1977).

Works on specific areas of Native American history include *Conquest: Montezuma, Cortés, and the Fall of Old Mexico* by Hugh Thomas (Simon & Schuster, 1995), *A Good Year to Die: The Story of the Great Sioux War* by Charles M. Robinson III (Random House, 1995), *The Lance and the Shield: The Life and Times of Sitting Bull* by Robert M. Utley (Ballantine, 1995), Ralph K. Andrist's *Long Death: The Last Days of the Plains Indians* (Macmillan, 1993), James C. Olson's *Red Cloud and the Sioux Problem* (University of Nebraska Press, 1965), Merrill D. Beal's *I Will Fight No More Forever: Chief Joseph and the Nez Perce War* (University of Washington Press, 1963), Alvin Josephy's *The Nez Perce Indians and the Opening of the Northwest* (University of Nebraska Press, 1979), and *Once They Moved Like the Wind: Cochise, Geronimo, and the Apache Wars* by David Roberts (Simon & Schuster, 1993). Geronimo's own autobiography, *Geronimo: Story of His Life* (Corner House, 1973), tells of the last Apache defeat in his own words.

Finally, some recent books written for young people include:

Joseph Bruchac, *A Boy Called Slow: The True Story of Sitting Bull,* illus. Rocco Baviara (Putnam, 1995)

Clifton Cox, *The Forgotten Heroes: The Story of the Buffalo Soldiers* (Scholastic, 1996)

Russell Freedman, *Cowboys of the Wild West* (Houghton Mifflin, 1985)

William Loren Katz, *Black Women of the Old West* (Simon & Schuster, 1995)

Andrea Davis Pinkney, *Bill Pickett: Rodeo Ridin' Cowboy,* illus. Brian Pinkney (Harcourt, Brace, 1996)

Judith S. St. George, *To See with the Heart: The Life of Sitting Bull* (Putnam, 1996)

INDEX

Apache, 34, 55, 57, 60
Arapaho, 41
Army, U.S., 34, 38, 41, 45, 46, 50, 54, 55
Aztec, 10

Bascom, George, 55
Beckwourth, Jim, 14, 15
Black Kettle, 41
Bonga, George, 16, 17
Bonga, Stephen, 16, 17
Bozeman Trail, 45
Brown, Clara, 30
Buck, Rufus, 23
Butler, Luticcia Parsons, 32

Cheyenne, 41
Chippewa, 17, 58
Chivington, Col. John M., 41
Civil War, 18, 34, 41, 42, 55
Clark, William, 53
Cloud, Kitty, 58
Coacoochee, 38
Cochise, 55, 57
Comanche, 41
Congress, U.S., 34
Conley, Elvira, 32
Constitution, U.S., Fourteenth Amendment to, 49
Cortés, Hernando, 10
Crazy Horse, 46
Creek, 23, 38
Crow, 45
Custer, Col. George, 46

Dart, Isom, 20
Dundy, Elmer, 49

Earp, Wyatt, 21
Enlightenment, 13

Fields, Mary, 31
Fletcher, Diana, 59
French Revolution, 13

Geronimo, 34, 56, 57
gold rush, 26
Goldsby, Crawford, 22
Grant, Ulysses S., 26, 42

Hayes, Rutherford B., 26
Hin-mah-too-yah-lat-kekht, 52, 53
Hodges, Ben, 21
Horn, Tom, 20
Horse, John, 38, 39
Howard, Gen. Oliver, 54
Huddleston, Ned, 20

Indian Removal Act (1830), 37

Jack, Captain, 50, 51
Jesup, Gen. Thomas, 38
Joseph, Chief, 52–54
Juanita, 59
Juh, 34

Kintpuash, 50, 51
Kiowa, 41, 59

Lakota, 41, 45, 46, 49, 60
Lee, Robert E., 42
Lewis, Edmonia, 58
Lewis and Clark expedition, 53
Lincoln, Abraham, 42
Little Bighorn, battle of, 46
Little Raven, 40, 41
Looking Glass, 54
Love, Nat, 18–19

Manuelita, 59
Mason, Biddy, 28–30
Masterson, Bat, 21
Modoc, 50
Monroe, George, 26
Montezuma, 10

Nana, 34
Napoleon, Emperor, 13
Navaho, 59
Nez Perce, 53–54

Oberlin College, 58
Ojibwa, 17
Ollokot, 54
Outina, 36

Parker, Ely, 42, 43
Parker, Isaac, 22–24
Pawnee, 45
Pickett, Bill, 60, 61
Pikes Peak gold rush, 41
Plains Indians, 41
Pocahontas, 11
Ponca, 49
Powhatan, 11

Reaves, Bass, 24, 25
Red Cloud, 44, 45
Revolutionary War, 34
Rocky Mountain Fur Company, 14
Rolfe, John, 11

Seminole, 38, 39, 58
Seneca, 42
Sherman, Gen. William Tecumseh, 26
Shoshone, 45
Sioux, 22
Sitting Bull, 46, 47, 54
Smith, Captain John, 11
Standing Bear, 48, 49

Taylor, John, 58
Tibbles, Thomas Henry, 49
Timucuan, 36
Toohoolhoolzote, 54
Toussaint L'Ouverture, 12, 13

Ute, 45, 58

Virginia Company, 11

War of 1812, 34
Wildfire, 58
Williams, Cathy, 33
Williams, Moses, 34, 35